Schizophrenic Sapiosexual

DECEMBER ATLAS

December Atlas
Schizophrenic Sapiosexual

Book Layout:
Jen Henderson at Wild Words Formatting

Front Cover and Book Layout Design:
Rebecacovers-Fivver

Printed in the USA
Schizophrenic Sapiosexual/Christine Martinez-1st Ed.
ISBN: 978-0-578-35231-2
Library of Congress Control Number: 2022900625

Connect with author:
DecemberAtlas.Poetess@gmail.com

Dedications

To my daughter Lyric,

I knew you were something special from the moment I held you in my arms. Born after so much heartache, you made me forget the world and remember how it was that a poet is supposed to view life. The more that you have grown the more I am sure that you were made to love hard and to be a warrior. In life you will go through many stages of love and heartache. Do not let what seems like failure hinder you from showing the world how truly amazing you are. Continue to always show how loving and kind you can be to others, in whatever walk of life they may present themselves. Lyric, you have the ability to see the good and tenderness in others and nurture it, this is your strength. I pray that you always practice this because it is through your actions that others will see you in the same light I do. They will recognize that you are truly a genuine person worthy of so much love. I hope that you continue to nurture your creativity and share your artistry with others. I believe you are one of my greatest works, afterall you were named for the lyrics in poetry and I am proud to be your mother. May you take my steps in going after my dreams as an example in your own life and run towards your goals. My wish for you is that you always stay true to yourself and be proud of who you are. You will always be a work in progress, just be sure to learn from every mistake and grow with every chapter in your life. I love you forever, plus one.

To my son Eros,

They say that a son is a mother's anchor and you my dear are just that. You are the heart of our little family, always full of love and light. I am thankful that I was blessed with such a beautiful human to call my son. When I named you after Cupid I had no idea just how true your name would be to your personality. You show me every day that there is so much beauty and love to add to the world. I had many doubts for so long that I would not know what true love felt like. However, you have shown me that there is no love like that of a son for his mother and that is true love. There are so many moments you've helped me to remember when my self love or confidence falters there will always be someone that loves me no matter what. May you never let go of your loving and accepting nature because so many people need someone like you in their lives. There will be many who will try to tear you down and cause you heart break and sadness. Do not be discouraged in these moments my dear because you are strong. These are the tests in life that you will need to learn that it is okay to feel your emotions but you must always retain your positivity in the end. Your outlook on your own life is the only opinion that matters and you must always keep an unmovable self love.

Continue to be the boy who brings love and light into the lives of others and the same will come back to you as it has done so already. I love you forever, plus one.

Remember my children the most
important lesson I could share with you is this,
'Change nothing about yourself but your clothes.'

Letter from the Author

I was born in Perth Amboy New Jersey to Hispanic parents and am one of three children, with a twin sister and an older brother. Growing up, I would often compare myself to my siblings as well as peers. I fell short of the athletic prowess that my twin had and was not as scholarly as my older brother. However, upon entering a poetry program in school, I found my voice and my passion. My journey began by studying poetry at arts high schools and college, then joining poetry programs after school. My mentors would tell me "You write the way you should speak and vice versa." Poetry became the only way I could properly express myself and communicate; I had found that it was my native language. Writing for me was, and is, a way to put reality into perspective while bringing fantasy to life. It helped me to see that I did not "fall short" of anything, as I had originally thought. For me, strength was in my imagination and it poured out of my pen onto the page. As an adult I wanted to share this with future generations of poets and began to teach poetry to children in the same after-school programs I had attended. Being a poet for so long I have learned a writer should always explore life through constant metaphors while attempting to see more than what is obvious. This is what I wanted to teach my students while exploring forms of poetry they may not otherwise learn in an every-day classroom. When I saw that learning these new forms of expression helped these children to grow, I finally decided to publish the book I had always wanted to.

Through these experiences is how I have gained the confidence to produce my book, Schizophrenic Sapiosexual. There are moments and things in this world that deserve to be seen for how beautiful they truly are. One way to immortalize them is through the written word. Poetry is the translator for this and it is needed for those who wish to relay their innermost thoughts and views that need understanding. So, I encourage my readers to do just that, attempt to see the world from a different light. Make beauty out of what they can if possible and write about it. Explore the connections we have with everyone and everything around us while appreciating the mass metaphor we live in. By writing this book, I hope to share with you my journey through the one emotion we have all felt in one way or another, love. Whether it be a love that was not returned, the love of a friend or family member, or the most difficult self love, we have all experienced it's joys and pains. My hope for you as the reader is that this book resonates with you. Let your emotions shine through your art and through your own voice and find the same strength I did when experiencing life through a ballpoint pen.

My last words to you are to remember to love no matter what and to be patient in a world on fire.

December Atlas

Table of Contents

Chapter 3: Storge
(Familial Love)

Chapter 4: Philautia
(Self Love)

When deciding to write this book, I thought about what I wanted to share with you. The first thing that stood out to me was an emotion everyone feels at one point or another; love. In poetry and other pieces of literature, love is portrayed as a grand and wonderful thing. Most people want to read about the fantastical version of it, but what about the different types of this emotion? Those different types of love, or what we think is love, are the themes I want you to read about and feel while reading my book. I wanted to dive into more than just the romantic side of love. This is where Schizophrenic Sapiosexual was born; a book that explores the illusion, delusions, and realities of love.

Taking it one step further, the chapters have been ordered in such a way reflecting how I believe we all experience these types of love. If only love were further explored or experienced more freely then, maybe, this book would be ordered differently. Until then, this is a minor look into the heart of one poet's view of love.

CHAPTER 1

Erotica Pragma

(Lust and Lasting Love)

Eros is a passionate type of love; lust,
if you will. It represents a feeling that often
causes us to lose control over ourselves.

Pragma is the type of love that is
worked on and we have patience with
because we want it to last a lifetime.

I believe eros/lust is a great mix of pleasure and pain
that everyone experiences often. Coincidentally, it is
also a feeling people would like to keep and work on
feeling throughout the entirety of their relationships
and life. Lust is the type of love that inspires us most
often. It becomes a feeling of euphoria that can elevate
the senses in a way nothing else can. If I could live in
lust for eternity, I'd gladly writhe in the pain it causes
me. Feeling the goosebumps and butterflies that make
my skin crawl from this type of love is what I crave.

Cocaine Connoisseur

Craving conversation like a cocaine connoisseur, I need a hit
but there are standards and only one brand will do
Your aesthetic is sedative enough to
inject intravenous intimacy into me
So heat up the white noise and
pour the parlay into me
I want to get high on your dialect
and appreciate every gram of you until what's left
are the crumbs of the chemistry we had
I've left too many 80's for 20's in my time
but I'll keep it 100 for you
Cutting out the bullshit and white lies so these
rows of white lines can only be filled by
OUR POETRY
Ready to inhale and intoxicate
so my subject moves with your predicate
On waves of dopamine
And it's dope I mean
being on this speedball induced monologue
about our love
That's the kind of feeling I fear
because I've never been good with heights
But as I suck the synonyms of the sin I'm in off my teeth
the craving grows
This love is euphoric and I'm for it
because a connoisseur knows
It's hard to find that pure 'ish'

The kind of rock that's got your back when you need it
How I love when my soliloquies turn to you and me
Wrapped in text
Sleeping under a sky full of definitions
Knowing our verbal exchange
is the only snow I want to taste on my tongue
With all kinds of conversation that leave me numb
and addicted
I could spend every day looking
for the 8-ball that leads me to you
and never feel it's wasted
I've graduated grams and ounce Phd
With you as my major
Always researching because loving you
is no minor thing
And I'd like to further my career
But I continue craving conversation
Feeding into 'Charlie's' hallucinations
Just to say I had you once
Before Withdrawal

Big Bang

When my children ask me what the Big Bang was, I will tell them "It's what happened when you and I locked eyes for the first time walking outside of the art gallery, even if it was just to cross the street and you needed to make sure I stayed within the lines while I wanted to color outside of them and make a beautiful picture."

When they ask me what the Big Bang was, I'll tell them "It was the first time we held hands and I felt a connection. The same one you told me was there when you knew you wanted to spend all your Sundays with me and a conversation with God." Those Sundays when the only things that mattered were syrup kisses, coffee-creamer love, and just enough background noise to keep us focusing harder on each other. Me reading the funnies that weren't that funny and your nose burrowed in the couch, waiting to catch my next move. It was the way you shined brighter than the UV glow of the paint I used to tell our future that night. I was all nerves. Let's be honest; I'm always all nerves when it comes to you because I can't be in love with you. How can I be in something like that? I am not made to swim; and, love is not a pool to play in.

When they ask me what the Big Bang was, I'll tell them "It's when I learned to float because with you, I am not in-love. We are love, surrounding life like oceans of what is right and natural, changing the ripples within our memories like second nature to our chakras. The past is planning our futures for us; had we known about these other lives, reincarnation wouldn't be the event planner to reinstating our old souls' bond.

When they ask me what the Big Bang was, shit, I'll tell them "Those were the nights they wondered why the monsters under their beds were so loud."

Then, when they say they thought the Big Bang was about science and chemistry, I'll tell them they were absolutely right. If they could only see the chemistry we made with poets and patrons in September. Alchemists trying to create the perfect covalent bond, or the way science worked on the soccer field; when gravity pulled our atoms closer to share our electrons because after breaking, we could only gain stability together.

My hypothesis: when my nucleus split there was no restoring me until that Big Bang, when your atoms gave me stability.

Argentine Tango

It's our Wednesday night tryst.
In between you and I
Your left and my thigh
There's shared history
Our story is like the Argentinian Tango.
We've weaved in and out,
In and out,
In and out,
Of each other's consciousness
You've slathered my dreams
With
Hot
Buttery passion
That slides down the creases in my brain,
Clogging all common sense.
While I've left incessant images
Of the poetry we bred,
Swaying intimately with your REM cycle.
Your left and my thigh have been in *Rueda*,
Yet only on Wednesdays do we meet
En Media Luna
To continue dancing *Quebrada* into a new
History of a second preformed,
Where our Wednesday-night tryst becomes a
Daily reminder of how we've loved each other

A Falling Poet

Which do you find sexier, your poetry or me?

Would you get high from stanzas stroking the line or would you prefer stroking me?

I find the time you take for lines to develop is taking mine; and, if these soliloquies were meant to be, then why are you not speaking my language?

I can fit my A's with your E's, but no I's with your U's on any given couplet.

Is that the way we make poetry together; is that how we'd spend our last days?

I'd tell you how my last supper would consist of poems and rhymes. How I'd taste the salt and pepper garnished on every word and the consonants my aperitif just to get my ears ready to listen to the main course of those stanzas.

Wonder if it were a broiled sonnet of our life gone, a rye or a pouched pantoum of this long-lost love. Possibly a smoked side of drama I never knew I'd always known… in the form of prose poetry.

See, my punishment of the last light was loving the limelight too little. Never craved too much, never asked much less. Why was I a happy medium?

Content with life and all its flaws, stabbed my paper with my pen and ate the meaty pieces raw so I could taste what was wrong and what was right with that book-savvy cat. Then went on to the sweet dessert of vowels A'ing and O'ing into my mouth; and, for every spot they hit, I'd salivate at the creativity dripping from my executioner's hand.

See, I devoured our last meal with a quill pen, a paper napkin, and intentions of serving every sentence given; yet, what was I given?

An aubade of how your poetry left you in the middle of writers' block on the corner of permanent silence. Well, all your well-known poets and poetry can stand aside as I walk away with the poetry you could have made with me.

Bustelo and Books

We break fast with Bustelo and books in separate spaces
thinking of the ways our words court each other. How
inflection and misdirection could make for a good
rendezvous when no one is truly listening

Carefully placed words planning ambush attacks
Create mental climaxes releasing tension with this
stimulating connection
Leaving these ellipses stroking new thoughts of explicit
frustrations leading to mental masturbation

I want to paint myself over with your soul
Look in the mirror and see nothing but the poetry we
make from our conversations and misadventures with
punctuation

Let me live within these brackets laid between your
embrace
And, though we're only on the preface we convert to coins
upon the tracks
Where our trains of thought run their two cents
Extending interests like pressed pennies

From monologues to soliloquies
We imprint on each other's parenthesis
Leaving the rest of our books on the outside

Call me your Mary Jane
I'll be blunt
The signs crossed my mind more than a Catholic in church
I'd let my body be your false idol

We can share sin together making mayhem from
metaphors
While we dance between the sheets
Of a Prose Piece we discovered
On a night of full moons and sailors dreams

Where you crave dry land and a place to let our words
flow behind backs
Knowing these thoughts move forward while keeping our
lungs still
I swear you are the devil's tool

Sent to tempt my pen into writing aubades
Because, while words vibrate within me
The sun is rising and
It pains me to hear "goodbyes"

When those "love-me-tender" lips tell me things
That don't match the words that escape them
We're torn like the drafts of our first shared piece

A balance between raw and real
Pretend and present
So, we wait

For the mornings where the Bustelo and books
Can remind us of the best bitter stories we shared
Over passenger side salads and avocado toast

Rose Buds

He told me I tasted of key lime

My inner thighs, the pathway to the most

Delightfully tart fruit

He ever pressed lip and tongue upon

The folds of my skin were to him, like the cracks in time

That every happy recollection had fallen through

He asked me if he "could take a look down memory lane?"

My eyes would be his looking glass.

"We would see our futures."

He said to me

"Let me be your groundwork and you my bed of roses;

I'd like for your blossoms to bloom against my skin."

So tenderly did he lay down his hoe

That made those blossoms bloom

& we thought;

"There shall be no better garden than this."

Honey Bees

She said she wanted to write stories between my legs
"Whisper sweet nothings" into my cave of wonder
I was no rival to her quick wit that got me wet when
she came at me on some other shit
Telling me how dirty talk meant tutorials about
how she'd touch me
Taking walks down memory lane; then, when her
fingers walked down my back, I'd call her name
And think of how it'd feel for her roots to be
planted within my womb
Where my body would water her branches that
reached outward just to touch me
I'd want to paint her poetry on my skin and practice
Morse code between the pages she played with
when thinking of story lines
That left my thighs stained with the honey she made
Pollinating my flower; this bee takes her time
She knows "a rose by any other name would [Not]
smell as sweet"
Soon, we greet each other with mango y miel nectar
Dancing in the middle of where the wind blows us
As random as four-leaf clovers, cleverly planned
by God when he made us all those years ago
It's a pretty storm that sways my emotions to the
branches of her evergreen
Where our story writes itself across my feminine
meadow

Delicately, written from side to side
Her hands create the silk-lined webs on each blade
of grass that covers my ground still blessed with
this morning's dew
This natural occurrence mother nature called for
When we meet and the emotional erosion leaves us
naked needing each other
I understand she needed to write her story so my
legs left a presence wherever I traveled

Mis Grietas Están Llamando

Your breath creeps across the valley of my back
And moves my tender mountains
Closer towards your wet lips
Inviting me in.
Every summons personally delivered
To the erogenous areas of my existence
Nape of neck, small of back,
That wonderful place between my thighs, and
Oh,
As though you've been watching my fantasies
Crawled into my maiden head
Then mounted my carnal thoughts
Tus manos ir a explorer
A través de cada uno de mis grietas
As tremors consume my skin
No room for peace
This swollen earth succumbs to your requests
That dance just over a vulva now,
Waiting for an eruption
    De sus tierras reclamadas
Whispers brushing the grassland
Over the caldera
Like sensual dreams
    That swiftly fade away

1900

I'd play her skin like those ivory keys on his piano
With tunes that flow sweetly out of her mouth
The highest of jazz royalty could not compete as when the
ash of that lit cigarette is more than what can be smoked
I'd caress her
So, her body knows,
without letting a single particle drop,
I'd keep her broken pieces intact
Then pleasure the harmonies hitting her strings at the
proper pressure
Vibrating on octaves only the sweetest angels could hear
Because making music with her is celestial and Heaven
only knows where notes like these come from
Maybe the blind could share my view
When I read her body following the rise and fall of it
Catching the air outside her lungs
Inviting the world to share her existence
She gave me the butterflies and bees knees all at once
When she sat across the miles of bar that separated us
Her honey brown eyes watching the musical promenade I
just enjoyed paving in my thoughts
It's as if she were the ghost writer of my piano dance
daydreams
And, I think loving her must be like Hemmingway and
dumbbells
Like Baker and a bench-press
Her smooth jazz curves and heavyweight spirit

Make me want to act on the verbs and turn them into
muscle memory
Pressing her punctuation into my piano's prose
The rhythm's always different
Now, it mimics the love I'd find with an audience
Reading the crowd until one face sticks
Then, I can play those keys as long as her face reads
satisfied

Dangerous Poetry

Falling for the poet was no easy feat;
but, it was easy to fall at those feet as the words tumbled
off this artist's tongue and took a dive into your ears
whilst their stage presence dug tunnels into your pupils
trying to get you to see them properly
Then your days together begin with a sonnet's rise
shining brightly over your pens bringing co-authors to a
carnal cadence
Until afternoon aubades begin the unveiling of what this
feature would become
Ending under the monologue of your artistic performances
So, you sleep to escape this but wake up still running
On memories and fear,
Running with no partnered publication,
Running,
Hoping the sonnet will rise again
and you will rest on the poet's chest listening to the beat
of a new pantoum
Singing *1*,2,3,4…
2,5,4,6…
5,7,6,8
With enough repetition to embody your group piece
And the perfect number of new lines to breathe new life
into this poetry
Without tainting the page

—For Apis Mellifera

Ardent Author

He put his hands where her words were
Sat her blank page down upon his wooden desk
And began to write
Smoothed his hands
                    (Like parentheses)
Over her body
                    The secret behind the cloth
Then moving downward to a pause
Where a comma cupped her ass
And lingered like an ellipsis…
Up and down her thigh
Thinking of the next sentence
Before this one ended
                    He added a question to his narrative
By nibbling her neck
Where did the ellipsis lead?
Other than
The semicolon between her thighs
                    That blurred whether or not
This exchange of thought was the beginning or end
The final statement made
As plainly as the punctuation in her abdomen
All while his quotes tended her mouth
                    She'd ultimately hit the peak of his story

The Greatest Expectation

If I were to lose you, I'd go mad
Though mad is what I am now
With the air drunk in my lungs making my head spin with doubt
How could I have been so wrong
The ways I had chosen to sing my song have been in vain
While you've laid hidden for years
Why erupt now amidst the chaos
To make ruins with the words you drive into my body?
Becoming my narcotic
Giving me your love
Like intravenous serums for cancer patients
You make me better
Yet, I feel worse for it,
Why do I get to be better with you?
This cancer that attacks my immune system
Life Stage 4
It cannot be reversed, only remedied
Even that takes decisions
How do the twists of this reality stop?
When I do not drive at the wheel
But am only a passenger
Yet, still on my journey, you hitchhike your way onto the ride with me
Oozing honey

The same kind of sweet flavor that dances on the skin of
my thighs when tasting mango memories and sipping
secrets we share in chalices of conversation
You make me mad
In the way Finn craves Estella
Because around you I can only have great expectations
Because love isn't hard if you love hard
And last I spoke to Chet Baker he had it right
"You make me smile with my heart"
But, I still argue with Judy because I can't have you
"Do it again, do it again"
What is this blue madness that has me thinking back and
forth on swings under moonlight?
I pop pills to forget but your memory because it's too
strong
Like how we both want a touch more than a tease
I Never said I wouldn't spoil you too
Let's dance in the rain like two clichés on plagiarized
pages stolen from each other's books
Letting our ink bleed into the same chapters
With ill-drawn illustrations
"Yet, you're my favorite work of art"
Hung in the galleries of museums for ekphrastic poems to
bloom in our eyes
You make me mad and I need you to know this
You make me mad and I NEED YOU TO KNOW THIS.
But, Judy wants me to "do it again, do it again,"
Don't "do it again, do it again,"
I Need you to "do it again,
[please] do It again

CHAPTER 2

Unrequited

(Love Not Returned)

Unrequited love is one that evokes more sadness than satisfaction.

It is a love not returned.

Within this realm of love you can only feel alone. Comparable to reaching to the sun, there are nothing but negative repercussions when falling in love and not having it returned. Likewise, sometimes being the object of someone's unrequited love can be painful. These poems demonstrate what the consequences are for both sides. Love often ends with disappointment and pain many times before happiness is found. Going through these moments of despair only make the desired outcome more delicious if it is ever achieved.

Crucifixion

He said "Give me one last kiss. A way to say goodbye. I know you want to."

But, I am no one's last supper. I will not serve the last feast to the one who crucified me.

God didn't create me to suffer for his sins or lay waiting to be betrayed before your "cock" crowed three times. Recreating the resurrection of Lazarus inside my cave with his false idol.

And on the third thrust it rose again in fulfillment of his scripture.

Bathing in blood so that he was passed over to claim the first vacancy in my womb.

But what I bore, was a serpent's child, devoid of innocence and holding my tainted apple.

After this mockery of Moses partnered seas to drown his Pharaoh's staff in me. I was thought to be a Magdalene, when asking for the hand of God to absolve me of his sins.

Because that is what I represent now, HIS CARNAL SIN.

New and unexpected like that of our Lord's finest garden.

Damning to the life I knew before, like Eve I was blamed for this happening because no one acknowledges the snake he carried between his legs.

"Give me one last kiss;" this Judas said to me before sunrise. Moving closer to my face as I turned the other cheek to avoid this Baptism by fire. I scrambled through his grasp for "A way to say goodbye."

By nailing me to the bed he left holes in my courage and drove past my strength with his spear forcing all of my tears to escape.

I wondered what Peter would say at the gates when he arrived. Page 3,211,989 verse 1:12:20

"What have you to say of this, the 5 black prints on her left arm, the purple adornments you branded her legs with?"

My photo painted in the book of the dead, as evidence of his theft, was etched there on our bed. Legs… no pages spread open by him.

As his smirk rose with his member, his soul sank with my grace.

I lay on our bed crucified, thinking of the child in the next room then restored myself. Forgive he who trespassed against me, so that when we took our steps outside, I could deliver her from this evil.

—For he who forever changed me

Blue Love

Staring at your evaluations always seemed to hurt me.

Like a lemming, I followed your words straight off a cliff then fell away from you.

I'd lost my ability to be a leader, instead I followed your directions.

But they were written for someone else and now my heart is no longer blue.

I don't think I'll ever use that shade of love again because—it belongs to you only.

As much as I care, it never shows up in my test scores.

I always thought tests were useless anyway.

I'd rather memorize what made you smile than how I needed to answer the questions.

Because if I

A – answer too late,

B – answer without more than one syllable, or

C – all of the above;

I've failed.

So, what's the use in these tests and directions when I was made to work with my hands?

I've been your apprentice yet learned about myself .

I can say, I'm more ready for salary than this entry-level position you've stuck me in.

But, your blue designer uniform was simply a way to keep me from turning in my resignation. Though I'd have given anything to wear your shade of love for a lifetime career with a full partner's pension;

My heart could only play intern for so long

until I had to follow the lyrical lemmings that you sent my way then let it burn.

Because we can love hard but

it gets hard to stay when all the qualifications for the job are denied.

Left to be stored on a message rod with all my love post-it-notes proof.

Kept in one place and pierced together for a paper weight on your desk.

Fog

Sitting on separate shores fog grows between us
the cold breeze hits my shoulder.
Mimicking how my bed felt yesterday
as the oven from today's meal keeps his temper just as hot
as always.
There used to be a flow,
when things slid off us and we rose above them
because we both ran hot.
There was no lukewarm love
until our currents' situation changed.
All frustration crashing forward
Little secrets rising up causing condensation in both of us,
We were like thunderstorms.
Coming down on one another in fits of desperation,
while those beads of condensation hit our faces,
"como un agua cero."
But I had his arms for protection;
a personal raincoat,
and he had mine.
Waiting, open to cover him from the downpour
Until our words did the dancing since we were meant to
converge.
Creating this cloud,
the same one that birthed the fog we sit in now,
the same that gave us time, enough to find the calm
in the middle of our Coriolis conversation.
We ran ourselves in circles

between "he saids" and "she saids"

The "I felt" and "he felt."

Not knowing that this dance, serine as it was,

only brought up the missing pieces then caused a downfall.

Where with great speed we lost our shared footing,

saw this dance was a battle,

and became a hurricane.

Fighting for whose words could travel fastest to the center eye,

at the core of which used to be love.

But our reach was not long enough to meet in the middle.

With all the air we'd blown out, we created a front we needed to confront.

We'd have to weather it before the next storm.

There were bound to be more storms,

And lightning.

Where rain from our overflowing orifices spawned by icy emotions

Then transferred positive charges.

One to reignite the spark we'd lost in that fog.

Why not sit in the mist together knowing

there was always the lightning to look forward to.

A reminder of beauty in the wake of storms

Lady Remix

Lost the emotions going back-and-forth in-and-out of ears
and hearts.
She's flossin' but can't get the dance down.
This DJ can't get the music out.
The melodies and rhythms living in her head
are scales of Romeo and Juliet,
fire.
Her lyrics divinely tell stories of the sacred.
Not getting past the chorus and bridge where the notes
change, and
I can't tell if this track just wants to play on.
While we're dancing to the same song,
she takes the lead.
Her fingers travel like needles on vinyl,
Burning tracks from the sound booth to
the radio
Givin' mixed signals but they can't reach my stereo.
She loves in the way she loves a remix.
Where she marries all the songs she's fixed.
Her lyrics are handsome but problems with static on the
station make for patchwork communication.
The best DJ you've never heard with indecipherable
spoken word.
Remix bought all the AP's and underground tapes, even
managed to learn some lines
But the best DJ's have most difficult rhymes,
I'd put my heart on her turntable if she'd give me a spin
and make this collaboration a permanent thing

Rotten Apples

The yellow/brown aging skin
Is what they see
It's not that rose red leather jacket they all wear
Before they've been used
But the mob of people forgets
Him… or… her
That Apple-store clerk who made us
So, imperfect,
reminds me of The Alchemist
Searching for his personal legend
Or, better still, Maria
And her *11 minutes*
So, I, I take hold of my aging skin
Right from the first seed
To the branch I Chose to leap off
To hell with those little Red Dresses
I want them to be Green with envy
Even if I stay
At the bottom
      This will be my journey
        A half-beaten… Half-Eaten
        Aging core
Hating my dear Apple-store clerk

          until he makes me his rose cider

Just the Wife

I am not my ring
I am not your trophy
I am more than just "the wife"
I am an opinion
An attitude
A personality
The curves throughout my body were not decided upon
When you chose me
They were molded throughout countless trials
I've had to endure
And the mountains I've had to climb
I am more than just "the wife"
I have made my feminine skin impenetrable
With all the scenes I've seen and been through
I have widened my stance after every birth
In order to stand
TALLER
Than the moments I've wanted to run and hide from
To be someone
They can look up to
I am not your trophy
There are more complexities within my persona
Then Quantum Theory
Learn about me
Unravel the equations behind my eyes
So That you remember who was there before the prefix
When we mixed

Like sugar water making our lives sweeter
I am an opinion
The reference log you went to when you had doubts
The debate that you sought when you needed to be humbled
And reminded that you live for a challenge
I have seen you at your worst and have loved you then
I have shown you my "rock bottom"
And trusted in the partnership we'd made
Not doubting you wouldn't climb higher without me
Because my arms were made for more than holding our children
They were built for the weight of the world
And my shoulders were not just for comfort
They were what balanced my beautiful mind
Atop my temple of worship
Because
I am not my ring
I am not a prefix
I am more than Your Last Name

Half-Priced Husband

Dear husband,

When I sent you to the grocery store, I asked you to pick up paper towels. I said, "I'd like a 10 pack of bounty. I needed a quicker picker upper."

Instead, you came back with 10 digits for booty because you were quicker to pick her up for a good time.

I told you going down aisle 6 you'd be able to find the cookies our kids like. Instead, you went down her gingerbread legs and tasted her royal icing while crushing the family pack.

See, you've taught me never to let a man do the shopping. Because, when I asked for fruit you grabbed her peach; while looking for cherries, you popped hers; and dammit, I always wondered why the bananas you got were still so hard.

Then again, I should've known. No man volunteers to go shopping unless he's looking for someone... I mean, something to eat.

Yet, I trusted you to be like our floor cleaner, Fabuloso. When really you were more Mr. Clean-break, leaving your last Jamima dripping in aisle 5 laying next to Ms.Crocker after a threesome. Even now, you keep on walking looking for something more satisfying.

Tell me, when did I stop being so mm,mm,good enough for you to sip on? Or, did you think I was part of a variety pack?

Funny how walking down the frozen aisle you could find my heart next to a hungry man, but I always came home for dinner.

You, husband, well you seem to be partial to cheaper snacks because once you popped you just couldn't stop. That's when I realized you were like soap.

Loved to be on everyone you touch but slippery enough to get past my suspicion.

It wasn't until they came to collect their points for a free holiday dick that my old receipts came into play. Connected to coupons I used and some I'd never noticed, like the 'buy one get some' that expired back in September, a shame that wasn't on the receipt's information. At the time, I thought I made it like a bandit; but turns out, nothing's worse than a half-priced husband.

Rose Colored

You said you saw my true colors
But never took your rose colored glasses off
See, I am the same woman you met long ago;
I am still flawed
Just as God made me.
I am still scarred
With permanent reminders of the past
And am still in-love.
But those glasses,
The ones you wore so fashionably,
They changed my true colors,
They did not show my Blues
Until you took them off And showed your green-eyed
ways,
Yet I am still in-love.
You are my Blinders
*A*sking me to stay focused
Only keeping my eyes on you
But, when yo*u* see without those lenses,
The yellow fear of losing this becomes
Brighter than you can handle
So, those spectacles you live by protect you
From a love that can be messy
And a woman who is loyal

Flint

"I found the day wonderful after the sunlight hit your
cheek in just the right way,"
Is what his eyes said to me
While yours say
"I plan to conquer you and plant my flag"

Contrast and conflict in this courtship
The movement of present and memories collide
While I try to decipher the problem with Our steel
These games of touch and touché that we play can satisfy
me for the moment
But moments need to be woven to make Time…

Go On

I live on the food, thought, and carnal pleasures
They bring me
But memories are memories
The distant recordings of how he walked down my back
with his hands
And dove into my ilium
Haunt the goosebumps Standing between my legs
Descriptions of what he'd love to do to me
Would …Mimic …the need that jumps off my pubis
And begin to slowly approach my limbic system
That's how I like it

Seducir mi cerebro
Antes de mi cuerpo

40

But we are strangers and your hands create the touché
To the touch I crave
Will I feel my fountain *overflow* to the pain of paying the
toll for affection
Or, will this spark ultimately ignite and cause her to weep
To calm the flames? Please

> *Seducir mi cerebro*
> *Antes de mi cuerpo*

Charlatan

There is an imposter sleeping in my bed
Trade it in for a new one
That feeling of sandpaper against my skin
Is Not the
>   Caress
I remember

Lies grow
Weaving wonderfully from under this tongue
Lying in that warm hole in my ear
That imposter is CrAyONed onto me
A gritty line
Breaks in every inch or so
Synthetically imprinted between my thighs
Like the crayon there are pieces missing
It's more like the Triatominae
>   Hiding under my pillow
>   Waiting for a Kiss
>   This imposter
The UNnecessary fitted sheet in the middle of a heat wave
Envelopes me in this water
Enjoying the space while I'm
>   Settled

My lips crack and bleed
Kissing a Dried Verse
even Adam Fought for love
But as my thighs become

Scratch Posts
For him and his HEAD to
Claw At
They've stained my maiden head and heart
        with
Unrequited

Poorly Printed

I'd like to settle into your fairytale of affection
To be an avid reader, start playing fact or fiction

To have love not lived on chapters but pages
Not short stories but one cohesive novel

The kind read in meadows under a purple sky
And be smitten by your bees knees

A rare mellifera apis
Landed on page five, line nineteen

It reminded me of when
I'd sit next to your spine and rely on your cover for support

My greatest protection were your pages
And you were the only author who owned my ears

But loving a fantasy is not the same as living a romance
These two genres don't blend as well as we thought

The amount of editing we'd have to perform is never-ending
And, we both want to publish one day

Through these outlines, we're stung by the facts laid out in
our first draft
A rough write of a passage that was left incomplete

Then after falling asleep in between your chapters,
Your binding began to come undone,

I'd not taken care of your first edition as I should have
So, you chose to keep chapters hidden.

Those little vignettes left nothing but silhouettes
Of what our full story could've been

As the reader, I could only assume your writer's intention
Though all stories were interpreted differently

I wanted to know your author's purpose,
Something we never got to explore.

Now in my library,
Looking at the shelves that used to house our mutual
desires
I sit
Window open

Waiting for that same bee to land on another page of
pleasant memories
Wishing your new cover wasn't so blue

But your work is copyrighted,
I can no longer twist your words into happier themes

Ones where we are the protagonists
Advocates for the ardent love we created

Treating poetry like prayer,
sacred and sanctified

That should have been our story

CHAPTER 3

Storge

(Familial Love)

Storge, a love we are hardwired to feel.

This love is well-known to all of us, it is the familial love. Something associated at first with parents and children. This chapter is filled with things I could never figure out how to say out loud. A memoir of my feelings as a child and a mother to my own children. There are moments as a parent connecting with my little ones that remind me of the things I so desperately needed to communicate when I was younger, but could not. Poetry is my only interpreter when trying to share my thoughts and I can only hope that this chapter resonates with a few choice readers.

Baseball Cards for the Dead

He comes again to name his best player's cards
It's not the mint condition ones that are the most valuable
But the ones that are broken in
Handled with love and stained with life
Each player's card a testimony to how great his coaching
is
Teaching his team to appreciate the game of life
Through practices that last forever
From the minor leagues starting in God's home field to the
days he lets us spread our wings and choose our own
players, creating a new family for the home team

The lord has christened you today
A mint-collectible card
With stats dating back to 1958
Getting started in the minors and following your skills to
the special forces in preparation for the real game
1982 you stepped into the majors taking your chance at
besting a new player and had your first taste of home
when you tied the knot and made your team name official.
Then, having that taste of victory the Lord decided you
could handle more players and began his additions in 1984
and a second expansion in 1987
That's when the first cracks of your career took off
breaking open the laminate seal letting your card truly
breathe
Every season only improved

Then your 50th year
With a fly ball made
Two hands on the bat and you controlling the winds
You felt what it was to be an angel in the outfield
Later on watching hopes and dreams light up the sky with
the team's future generations
Some waiting with T-balls in hand
To be taught by you
Other's just content to sit by your side at home plate and
enjoy the game with you
22,995 days of practice and playing ball
And it is now that he's called you to the hall of fame
Ushered by love and kisses from your biggest fan
Leaving behind the baseball card of an MVP that we've
all come to admire because it is not the most pristine
player who holds the most value
But the one who took chances, made mistakes, and played
hard ball until he finally made it to the greatest team in
God's kingdom

—For my father, Ruben Martinez. I hope I made you
proud this once.

Eyes

Hers were the eyes of God
Every little wrinkle and roll
In my skin she observed
Was memorized the day I was born
Down to the birthmark on my
Left
No…right foot
A cry to say "I need you" was answered
By the diamond studded magenta lips
That kissed the pains away
And the cotton colored spots that lay on her hands
That now blend in with my back
Told me that my night terrors had been defeated
After eating the years too quickly
I begin to feel full and tell her
It's not possible
For a fossil to blend in with the living.
What did I know?
Now that I've enjoyed French seven-course cuisine
When I am more accustomed to the Latino flavor
I realized upon having my own little "Chuchi"
That hers were the eyes of God
And when I memorized the birthmarks
On "Chuchi's" right ear lobe and her Lower left leg
I saw that we were not extinct in the fact
We are merely
In danger

Not endangered
In danger of being underappreciated
Now the bold faced font that
Was etched onto my heart and womb that labels me
Mother
Burns with regret for sometimes forgetting
Even 'till this day
To tell her
"I appreciate you"
"I love you, Mami"

—For my mother, Carmen Martinez. For everything left unsaid.

Helmets & Space Travel

You were never meant for space travel
Wiping your tears
I'm seated next to your stuffed bear
& see your questions
Through the light of LED stars on the wall
It's visible how this
Misdirection
Hurts you
The world's been opened
Pulled

East   then   West

While you stand in the middle
Waiting for which way the compass sends you today
I'd wanted to give you the heavens
Instead you travel through two realms
From bikes and late bedtimes
To kisses and crafts
YOU WERE NEVER MEANT FOR SPACE TRAVEL
But having no choice in the matter
I can only equip you with a survival kit
Of reassurance and hope
With helmets of understanding
Hoping
One day
You can fit this head gear
When traveling between
Bikes and late bedtimes
And
Kisses and crafts

News

Crying clear tears onto my blue robe
He read the answer on my face
Pregnant and I had just ended his life
Where all dreams of blue uniforms
Were the thoughts of
Diapers and pins now the fun begins
Testimonies of "I'll be there for you"
Forced their ways into my ear
Like forceps bringing out the truth
"We" didn't want this.
I did.
The way he held me
Squeezed everything out
He aborted my life
For that second
A glimpse of what I was
Doing to him
Dreaming of the white stick
With black bold print
I made it through the night
While he still struggled in the dark
Waking to his imperfect voice box
Pumping out soft tunes of secondhand serenade
He was given a second chance
"We" didn't want this; he did.
Three tests later and an appointment for
Freedom on Independence Day

His fingerprints no longer matched my own
We learned how to forget
Unattached to the world
He found his breath again
While the underdeveloped
Umbilical cord stole mine

Our lives were no longer in sync
The burden was still
Too light for his broad shoulders
To feel
But the pitter-pat of footsteps
Followed my own to bed

My Guardian

Will you be my Michael?
Could we stop the confusion
And savor every line?
Forget about our foes, our woes,
Our arguments and crimes,
Let our triangular and circular
Emotions become congruent

Though different,
I'd like you to overlap with my views.
Like the writing on college cubicle walls
Make my image legible, concrete
And through the bulbs above me flicker
To be my guiding light.

The lonely first note on the page
Has yet to start its symphony.
Who will stop the conductor
From creating chaos?
As the melody was written
So, it shall be sung

Then, with the hymns
That I present
Will you be My Michael
Standing to the right of me
To hold my heart on high?

You can read the Bible
In my eyes
It lessens the lines
On my face
The clock is tightening
Skin
Soon I'll be outside myself
Please, slow down the
Seconds,
Help me stay within

Moving in all directions
I'm fresh spilt coffee
On cloth;
The color was never adjusted
For my hands to seem attractive;
They're still waiting for
Someone to hold

Will you be My Michael,
My atlas when all
Is lost,
My brail when I can't see
The solution,
My last thought
Before Heaven greets me?
Be my Michael!

Tausi's Bug

We weren't meant to meet this way
I'd planned on signing certificates not hallmark cards
The day we conceived the idea of you
I had devised a master plan
Once you were in your chrysalis, a detail was added to it
at every stage
When we'd learned you were present, your first holidays
and
Ways to hold you
Marched through my imagination
Each outfit and swaddle on display
Like fashion week in Paris
I'd create your crib's red carpet in my sketchbook
In hopes that if my roots could not hold you
Some part of me would

As your limbs lengthened
So did the space between us
Your chrysalis had begun to close and I could not break
through
Like your metamorphosis my plans changed
Going from natural foliage
To nurturing flower
I was going to be the extra petals you rested your tired
wings on
That would help me to bloom with you
And give you a place to develop color

Because no matter where you soar little butterfly
My roots will always be long enough to hold you

—For A.J.I, I love you no matter what and will always be
your Tausi.

Carmen's Soldier

Saying farewell, she rests her head on his casket
Her tears the pall that gift wrapped his body for this
heavenly relocation.
Emotions were fatigued, as Carmen whispered she'd "see
you soon"
then tried to remember where the subway tokens to your
life together had gone?
She would give anything to be your "Bahama Mama"
again, but time has been a tyrant to us
and she its saddest prisoner.
Sentenced to life without Papi, she'd give anything to be free.
We all came into this penitentiary together without a clue
on how to escape.
Learning how to serve time without him weighed her
down more than when they placed the flag in her hands
and thanked her for your service.
Carrying on the Martinez name hadn't been difficult, until
her soldier did not come home from the battle field riddled
with mines of explosive cancer.
For Carmen, he would receive the purple heart for his
bravery and courage when at the end of his war he did not
beg for mercy but for more kisses and her love.
Now, with the tears of past soldiers falling from the clouds
to cleanse the spot he lay in rest,
she hears the melody of the taps welcoming her American
Hero into the hereafter.
Where he sits with tokens for her as she sends her love
every night when hugging his side of the bed.

Monkey-Bar Blues

Time is fleeting
They are slowly growing up and away.
Those monkey-bar blues are no longer being sung.
There aren't any monsters in the dark, only in their
imaginations.
The real-life-story twists begin now,
when they enter the age of cyberspace and social solitude.
I fade into their backgrounds.
A screen saver in their lives,
only there when nothing else occupies them.
There was a moment when pretend campfires and under-
the-table tents kept us connected.
She would help set up quilt sleeping bags while
he would forage for snacks in the refrigerator forest.
They would share all their secrets by the fire of flashlights
while their eyes remained glued to me.
Mami.
I was their influencer, not Tik Tok, Hip Hop,
Or, the blue birds signing on Twitter.
Our time together was filled with family days and making
memories.
Now, all that're left are memories,
of a little girl who loved to play dress up in her mother's
clothes and a little boy who fell asleep to butterfly kisses
What I wouldn't give for those monkey-bar blues to play
again.

When Puerto Rican rhymes could heal scraped knees and freeze tag was taken too seriously.

The days when glow sticks provided the light for a family rave in the living room and no one could touch the elf who never stayed on his shelf.

The days when water, glitter and perfume were the secret ingredients to monster spray and sleeping with my stuffed animals made them feel protected.

Instead, I am too old to understand them or any teenaged problem for that matter.

Their popular point-of-view believes I was never a child, so, I couldn't understand

But I know

I know that when she comes to me crying over her first heartache

I will meet her by the swings with a pint of ice cream and open ears.

And, when he has his first crush,

I'll be his "wing-mom" by the slide with her Valentine's Day flowers

And when they have their own children, I will be ready to explain to them

That the monkey-bar blues don't last forever.

—For Lyric & Eros. I love you forever.

Sweaty Bug

It's like watching the ebb and flow of your spirit sitting in
the back seat of the SUV.
Head holding up the window while rain fills your cloudy eyes.
You'll never understand how much I *DO* understand.
Those slow songs mumbled under your breath
are the same sonatas that once put me to sleep the nights I
didn't feel heard.
Outcries of individuality are not appreciated when
painting rebellion on your sails.
But I am your most devout supporter.
On days you get lost in your Bermuda Triangle of pillows
and lay in that Dead Sea of emotion, my life rafts are here.
Ready to embrace you and navigate the rough seas together.
Sirens may sing to you a diatribe of unworthiness, trying
to pull you further into a deep-sea depression.
Though the pages of your captain's log might fill with
tears causing your confidence to float adrift but,
I still beg you.
Keep the clouds out of view so that you can see clearly.
No one can traverse this journey when focusing on the bad
weather
or getting lost in the siren's melancholy music.
Looking into the rearview mirror your perfect storms
catch my eye, then, I want to shift into reverse, follow the
wheels that turn in my mind and tell you
'Your's is a beautiful episode of life.'
You were never made to be liked.

Instead you were created to be loved, not to get lost at sea
by sadness.
You were made to revel in the storms.
Let the ebb pass and rise above the waves.
Twisting those sonatas into lullabies becoming
Amphitrite, queen of the ocean.
Calming the unruly sirens, finding yourself in that
triangle, while bringing life to those seas of emotion.

Lyric

The Lyric you are is more than words I give worth to
I birthed you
After nine months of pain
I heard you
Held you in my arms
And cried to
The soft tunes of cooing
You became my undoing
Changing my plans
As I carried you in my hands
Alone with no man
So we cried together
I cried for strength
you cried for me to be strong
While I held you tightly and
Our tears wrote this song
You're in all my chapters
To him you were just a verse
What makes this worse
Is that I couldn't reverse
The way your book was written
So I changed the story's foundation
And out of second-hand serenades
Came my greatest creation
Making you the first publication
The only Lyric I ever prayed for
The one my pen swayed for

Across paper
When writing letters to my maker
Playing chicken with faith
Letting my ego take weight
When I insisted he give me a daughter
I mean if he could walk on water
-Why not-?
Now, here we are each other's remedies;
You with his face but that heart, it's all me;
You've got it written in your blood
the story of true love
That never gets heard
About the Lyric worth more
than all my words

CHAPTER 4

Philautia

(Self Love)

Philautia is a difficult love to find and a
dangerous one to keep.

Self-love

This is the kind of love we have an overabundance of when
we are children, unaware of how the world works. We are
sure of ourselves and confident in who we are before we
know who that is exactly. Then, as we grow, the world
shows its ugly side and breaks us down via judgments and
standards. Self love is a funny thing because as it grows and
we nurture it, it can become our strength or our vice. In my
case, I am still a nomad in search of the kind of love that
fits me.

Still Editing

Down they fell,
the bloodstained pages of my heart
And what was once vivid
Is now muddied,
Sullied,
Worthless because
The words are illegible
Thoughts indecipherable
Emotions unbearable
Then, when opened,
My mouth is silent
A nickelodeon for the young to ignore and the old to use
as entertainment
This heart, a mime
Cage behind invisible walls
It's no wonder you don't see my intentions
To understand them myself is problematic
But, life the rabbit and his feet,
I pray luck is with my every step
On the way toward these discoveries
Excavating emotions to uncover the artifacts of my
antiquated love
Where care, cordial and courtship are a holy trinity that I
am proud to call my moral compass
Like the water we can't live without
These beliefs make up 70% of me

And, there needs to be trust before I can have my tryst
with pride
So, I continue to rewrite myself
Until the draft is complete and ready to share with my
readers.

Issues vs. the book

125lbs, 5'3 issue
34,28,38
This exclusive was incredible
Hair cascading past her ass
Emphasizing her curves
With that
Black background laying loose behind her
Damn! She was beautiful
With her
Mandarin-orange lips
Wet and plump
Begging to be bitten
Her olive eyes
Italicized by *Maybelline*
Maybe she was born with it
With the smooth café au lait skin that melted into
the mahogany spotted pillows
that adorned her chest
what was there, measured up to magazine standards
featured on the pages of her
greatest common factors
34,28,38
But that publication had so many issues to go through
So, I moved on to a more mature journalism
Moved to that 145lbs encyclopedia etcetera
with a history that stood 5'3 when opened
lips begging to be heard through audiobook

so, they kissed your eardrums with a voice
and olive eyes that observed every injustice
emphasized by the underlines of *Maybelline* tears under eyes
her volumes
34,33,45
Were not as prized as those old issues
And, the issue is,
She was me
So, you mean to say
Because my spine has widened
While my pages filled
I could no longer be the
Head liner
Now, I'd need to be thinner
A sinner
Sending false advertisements
With each photo op
I'm photoshopped
To fit your standard issue
But I am not an issue
I am a thesis, a dissertation
Something to look over more than once
Research my volumes
34,33,45
And you'll see
Maybe *Maybelline* saw I was born with it
And that's why she
Tried to make them believe otherwise
Because to her size

Does matter;
Because that's what society told her
It's the
34,33,45
That's become my greatest common feature
The way I see it
My 34,28,38
Changing from issues
To articles of growth
Made me proud to claim my volumes
Of womanly strength

Conversion Disorder

I have this condition where when stressed I change
It's a Jekyll and Hyde situation
See, it comes about whether or not I realize I'm stressed
Beginning with a tick in my face that curls my lip like I've
been fish hooked
But, what's the worry?
Sometimes, it travels to my eyes, closing them as though
shielding me from what I've seen.

I fell in-love with myself at an early age
Promising never to change
I made a pact with the mirror to always think outside of
the box my parents tried to bury me in
Every time they beat me with appliances and words;
Some Days more difficult than others
When bleeding that much everything is difficult
But, what's there to worry about; I got this

Once my facial tick got so violent, I had to punch my jaw
to get it to line up correctly
The pain was unbearable and that's when I noticed my
hand cramping
My tendons tightening like violin strings
But, the tick in my face was fierce and kept distracting me

In 2010 I sat in a courtroom after the 4th time my trial had
been adjourned
Waiting for my rapist
He walked into the room like a disoriented turtle
looking around then stole my sight
Like he tried to steal the pearl between my legs
While my child slept 4 ft in front of us
But, what's there to stress about? I got this

After twitching grabs hold of my face, turning towards
what's gone on,
I enter the tunnel
My eyesight narrows as the darkness hugs the rim of my
pupils
Strangling my point-of-view

I didn't realize I had undergone this conversion until 5
years ago
Sitting in a room of students
Drinking my lemon water
Because I wanted the waist of a "my size *Barbie*"
After being left by my husband,
I was in a daze thinking of how to take care of me and
mine
Telling myself "I've got this; I'm strong"

When my eye and face lose control,
I believe I can get through it;
Then my legs begin to fail,
My gate, wobbly as I walk
With the strength I worked so hard for gone,
I can't stand on my own

Those years ago, I found out that my Mr.
Had thrown me out and I had no home
But neither did my babies
So, walking from a couch to the other end of town
I took care of them because that's what a good mother did
Because wiping their tears
Was more comfort than shedding my own

But what's there to stress about
Walking with some help now struggling for balance
With more than a blindside
My tongue was converted to a tied cherry's stem
And, I can't sssstttttttop ssssttttutttering
But, what's there to be stressed about?
I I I've got this

The Other Hand

Pulling away from under his cloak
I see the hand that holds me back
The loose rock that falls onto me
They've beaten down the motivation that built the steps I
walked to arrive at his foot hold
How can I win in this arm wrestling match when the
opponent is infamous?
This is the hand I am dealt
The enemy I pray with at night
The one who supports my staff
Before I can see it slithers underneath my feet rather than
holding me up
It holds me in place
But I'd like to go down the river
Live by the flow and let go of these faults
To be like Moses and see we are all unclean
But this rival lives in leprosy
And misery loves company
These boulders and valleys that
Cradle my head are the same that hold my mistakes
That support my snakes
Hiding in the staff I leaned on before deciding to climb
Now raising my right to continue
I've forgotten what's left behind
The fault lines in my foundation
Are nothing more than new markets
A place to hook up a carabiner of faith

Come further from this cloak
And reach my summit
With the same enemy who helped me pray
Because now I'm humble and human
I am loved not leprous

Of All Conversations

There's a silhouetted woman
      Who pleases some eyes

The way her knees curve
Makes men tremble

Movement from her left index finger
Entices anyone looking closely enough

Slight fog forms on this silhouette
      Of the hairs raised due to frozen eyes

They look her way often

Walking in short strides

One pointed toe follows another

Careful
not to drop the conversation
Carried on lips
Outlined by whistling sorrow

The silhouetted woman
      has been disguised

She is a lady of the Algonquin table
Sapio by nature

Behind those lines of dimmed light
Your double-entendre killers
Are one-dimensional innocents
Seeking refuge in her mouth

The solid eyes melt from conversational heat
While her tongue dances sensually   with *dialect*
        Lengthening its strides
        Blocking passage to the whistle that follows her

Bending those perfectly curvaceous knees
Carrying the heavy Happy solitude of her *Left index finger*
Now trembling herself   as the conversation begins

An *initial intimate injection of inflection*
Can raise the hairs that question

This silhouetted woman wearer of many shadows

Depression Made Anew

Depression is setting in
Emotions deep
Pressing
Into my arms
Weighing heavily on my soul
Leaving invisible imprints at my core
While the rivulets run silently
Eroding my happiness while leaving my thoughts
deposited in places they don't belong;
I wonder how to mine for peace of mind
While stuck in the catacombs of cataclysmic
consciousness
How do I find the answers?
This obsession of proper emotional possession continues
towards depression
Like stalagmites from the ground up in my body until I am
hardened
Yet, like the maple, I wait for the positive pressure to
counteract
As my maple tears run down through my cracks
and turn into something worth it;
I am hardened from this inevitable erosion
Making me immobile
Stagnant
Stuck
Stalagmite
Where emotions press deep into my soul

Releasing those salt-water scars
Creating me
It's crystalized version
Now standing with the colors of resilience and pride

Porcu-guin

I always wanted to be a penguin
There are too many reasons why it should have been my
spirit animal
See, the way penguins work is this
The male when seeking a female
Builds a nest
Making sure to use only the best twigs, stones, and other
things it can find to make it look presentable enough for
its potential mate
Much like the female penguin
I, too, appreciate a solid foundation
To create love, life and a family
With twigs and stones being understanding, love and all
the other things in between
The male might also sing to the courted female, inviting
her to a ritualistic dance ceremony
Now, I too love a good song and dance
When true colors are being shown to me
There's nothing like someone who is not afraid to bear it
all before you in order to keep you to himself
Because, you see, most penguins are monogamous
Something I'd hoped to be since I was 16
When telling my mother much like these penguins my
partner would come showing
How much the way I loved him motivated a need to build
a life with me
Our own nest

Now as I age, I realize as much as I love my penguins
I am a porcupine
Misinterpreted and guarded
Porcupines in general are difficult
For so long it was believed that they shot their quills out
when they felt threatened
Like ammunition for an enemy
Instead, these animals are merely misconceived
Porcupines go out into the wild
Seeking compassion and partners
But in the process encounter predators
Much like the relationships I've lived through
So, they raise their quills mimicking the stripe of a skunk
just like that, I see that this porcupine and I both make
ourselves less attractive to these life-ending situations
But in the process shiver and chatter producing noises
while shedding our quills
I can see how my verbal quills can hurt potential mates
Even when they are not my intentions
Porcupines have a difficult courtship
Climbing into trees seeking the right one constantly
shedding quills until
The most resilient and matching mate comes
One who can maneuver these quills and see past the
disguise of fear
Trying to convince us we've each found our "forever"
I'd like to be a penguin, I guess
I'll have to accept that I am just a porcupine

Disease and Antidote

Once in the outside world we become infected.
The disease to please stigmas and critics finds its way into
our bloodstreams.
Breathing in this airborne pollution
Our neurological systems light up.
Electrons firing off at all points
mixing messages from our identities with the
advertisements that invade our organs.
It's a strange illness.
We've discovered this after realizing our own white blood
cells
couldn't fight off these insecurities injected into our veins.
Creating deformed self images and crippling egos,
the outcome is clear.
There is a pandemic and we all have different symptoms.
Like evolution, it's something that's gone undetected for
years.
Perfectionist parasites have bonded to our eyes like the
contacts we see through.
Blocking the natural beauty from being accepted
because our views have been blurred by man.
It's a designer disease that needs designer antibodies.
CONFIDENCE by *Calvin*
LIKEABILITY by *Lauren*
Or, even,
BEAUTY by *Brosius*
But, why not go natural?

Be our own lymph nodes.

Filter out all the fake, destroy all deception, and embrace who we are;

just imperfect pieces of cloth meant to stay that way.

Every birthmark a BIRTHRIGHT for individualism.

Allowing ourselves to be limited edition.

Throw away the guidelines to be good looking

The magazines to manliness and flyers of proper femininity

The diagnosis is simple

Vanity with side effects of insecurity

The antidote a mirror

Maintenance doses of self love and every once in a while

An overdose of acceptance

Self-Publish

Love the poet through pain and paper
Through turmoil and text
Fighting grammatical gremlins that grow in the mind
Pushing for immersion into the same
Ink-
Well,
The war starts now
Between mirror and metaphor
Plural and singular version of self
Is it the onomatopoeia of originality that is desired
Or a true memoir
written by the author
about the author
and solely for the author
That matter?
Creating a likeable character for an audience
Is not the most important task;
The real demand is in
pushing perception through a pen,
Letting sorrows become short stories,
Whispering words like weapons;
When learning how to become more than footnotes in life,
How do we please the publishers?
We become the publishers
Help the unrealized character make it to the shelf
And start our own genres
Living life in unexplored chapters

and preordered for the thrill readers
who are tired of the tales as old as time
Instead of reading self-help
Help yourself to publish authenticity
Then love the poet through pain and paper

Through turmoil and text,

Only pruning chapters to help them grow

Acknowledgments

Wilson, thank you for always believing in my work and pushing me to continue to hone my craft. Thank you for knowing when to use your red pen and when to allow my creativity to shine. Your influence on my writing as well as my life has been tremendous. The debates we've had about how a writer's message changes between the way it is read versus heard has elevated my work. You've constantly given me reason to explore my writing from multiple points of view. From our discussions about books, to sharing our own writing, even down to our pity parties, you have taught me an immense amount about just how powerful perspective can be. I am a more talented poet because of your insight. I am forever grateful to you for helping me realize what was once just a personal passion is so much more than that; it is something worthy of sharing with the world. If it were not for the confidence you have had in my ability as a writer I might still be only writing for myself instead of the audience I have found in so many people.

Thank you for being a sounding board for me and as always an inspiration.

Ryan, you have always been the person I relied on during the most difficult moments. I often looked to you when I needed comfort while I was lost or a calming word when I was hurt. For that I am in your debt. However, one thing I took from you that will always be a rule in my life is: "Never let the world see what you are feeling." So, it is because of this that I write, it is because of this that I can share my thoughts and feelings and let the audience interpret its own message. You are part of the reason that I am able to stay strong during moments when I should break, moments that should set me back. Your example as an older sibling has been something that has shown me how to find who I am meant to be and to be proud of it. Thank you for being the brother and friend that I have needed throughout those many moments.

Cyndi, my polar opposite, you are one person I have always admired. Your nurturing ways are what shaped my love for life. Living with someone who is, quite literally, another half of me can be truly eye-opening. When we were young, I only ever wanted to be you, to be "the good twin." I realize more as years go by that what I felt then was admiration. I admired you for being able to show the love and care I could only show in my writing. It was not until you told me once that you admire me for being true to myself that I began to love myself. Your words have had much more weight in my life than you could ever know. It is because of you that I continue to stay true to myself even when it is difficult. It is because of you that I can instill the idea of self-love to my children. There is no one who has shown more love for others whom I know than you. As such, it is only fitting that you were part of the influence of my poetic journey. Thank you for helping me to understand how to be me.

Jessica, you were a surprise in my life. Our meeting was a sign that my poetic future was bound to change. Bouncing poetic ideas off of each other while listening to each other's work is one of my favorite things. However, it was your constant checking in on my progress that enabled me to get to this point. If it were not for you showing me that attaining my dream of being an author of my own book rather than an add-on in someone else's was possible, this book would not exist. The saying goes "without bees there can be no honey." That is certainly true when referencing the creation of this book. Your drive to accomplish what you set out to do has poured into me and I am finally doing the same. Though there will be conflicts and opinions that will not always be in our favors, I will remain grateful for your influence and assistance. You have helped me to go beyond the familiar, from simple writing and performing to competing (a thing I never thought I would do.) Being an artist comes with much scrutiny, something you and I are no strangers to. Through our writing sessions, I have learned to consider all of that as a badge of honor. If there are no opinions, then there is no audience; and, isn't that why we write, for our audiences? Thank you for always listening to my poetry and indulging my metaphors, no matter what.

Carmen (Mom), while growing up, I could never speak to you about how I felt regarding so many things. However, I could always write to you. Ours was a classic mother/daughter relationship starting out on a rough note and now living within a calm one. I always knew you were a strong woman; but, becoming a mother myself, I can now see so much more. There were so many things I missed as a stubborn child that I can now appreciate as an adult. Hearing your stories, I see how we are more alike than I ever assumed. I understand where my resilience comes from and my ability to take care of what I need to in order to be a caring and loving mother. Your example has inspired me to become the best role model to my children that I can be and in publishing this book I hope to continue to be a good influence for them. I hope that they can look at me when they are older and say that their mother fought to achieve her dreams and did. When they do, I know that it will be because I had you to look up to. I am so grateful that I can not only call you my mother but now my friend and my support. I love you Mami.

www.ingramcontent.com/pod-product-compliance
Lightning Source LLC
La Vergne TN
LVHW041302080426
835510LV00009B/849